A Tribute to my Sista Girls...
You Ain't Grown Yet

BOSSHIA RAE

Best Read
PRODUCTIONS

A Tribute To My Sista Girls...You Ain't Grown Yet!

Copyright © 2015 by Bosshia Rae

All rights reserved. Printed in the United States of America. No part of this publication may be reproduced, stored in a retrieval system, or transmitted, in any form or by any means electronic, mechanical, photocopying, recording, or otherwise, without the prior written permission of the author except in the case of brief quotations embodied in critical articles and reviews.

ISBN-13: 978-0-692-53615-5
ISBN-10: 0692536159

Cover Design: Donna Osborn Clark at www.CreationByDonna.com

Layout and Interior Design: CreationsByDonna@gmail.com

Published by: Best Read Productions

This book is dedicated to my Mother, Arness F. Ivy and my aunt Janet M. Cook. These two women have taught me everything I know. Every aspect of this book comes from a talk that we've had, a laugh that we've shared and even a few fussings that they've given me. Because of them I am who I am today… a better MOTHER, a better WOMAN, and a better BRUNWYN. I would also like dedicate this book to ALL the ladies in my family. From my aunt Sissy all the way down to the youngest little lady of our family, my niece, sweet Sophie Claire Bear! Ya'll are some of the strongest, most beautiful sistas I know and I love you guys FOREVER. Last but sho not least, I'd like to dedicate this book to all the mothers out there who's making it happen for your kids on your own. I'm proud of you Sistas!

Acknowledgments

I would like to acknowledge all of my supporters! You guy's support and encouraging words has made publishing A Tribute To My Sista Girls… You Ain't Grown Yet, a whole lot easier! THANK YOU! I appreciate y'all!

Table of Contents

I'm Just Saying Sista Girl I 1

Your Own Woman 3

Attitude & Appearance 9

Find Your Own Groove 17

Gotta Keep Those Priorities Straight 23

Know Your Worth 31

For Me Or Nah 41

That Man, That Man Chile 47

Speak Up Girl 53

That Girls A Boss 59

Keep Squares Out Ya Circle 65

Picking Up The Pieces 73

I'm Just Saying Sista Girl II 81

Fashion Dos and Don'ts 83

A Gift From Bosshia (Just Write) 85

I'm Just Saying Sista Girl I

A lot of us get being an adult misconstrued with being "grown." We think that because we've reached a certain age or the fact that we have children means that we're grown. Well I'm here to tell you that's so not true! Being grown has absolutely nothing to do with age or the fact that we chose to laid down and make an adult decision to have a child. Being grown is a state of mind… a way of thinking. And in order to get in that state of mind you're going to have to go through some things. You're gonna have to cry. You're gonna have to get up, dust yourself off and keep it pushing when this cold world knocks you down. You'll know when you get there because your way of thinking is gonna completely change… you're gonna get to the point to where your whole perception of your family, yourself, your world… is totally different from what it used to be. It took me 32 years to become the "grown" woman that I am today. But Sistas believe me when I tell you, it wasn't easy!

Bosshia

Your Own Woman

When I was about 12 years old I can remember hearing two women whispering as I walked past them one day after school, "Girl you know her mama! The one who has the three little girls by the married man who live around the street." The other woman, "yeah, I know exactly who you're talking about. That's a damn shame too cause she's gonna be just like her momma… watch what I tell you." Now I've always been taught to stay in a child's place, so I did just that, and kept walking, pretending not to hear them. However, that was one conversation I would never forgot.

To this day, I still cannot understand why women of all people love to tear each other down constantly, when there are so many of us who could stand to be lifted up. SMH…That's so sad. Now why couldn't they have just asked, 'Brunwyn did you have a good day at school, or if you need any help with your homework, I'm available… keep your head up or something.' It took me a long time realize that I am my own person…, my own woman and there is no one in this world who can tell me who I am or am not, nor who I will or will not become but myself and the good Lord… that's it.

Sista, don't you ever allow someone to dictate or put a label on your life due to your upbringing. Not only is that a very unintelligent assumption, but it's just downright ridiculous. Yes, my mother was aware that my father was a married man before she chose to lay down with him. And yes, she had three beautiful children with him, every one of us conceived while he was married. But what does that have to do with me? I didn't ask to be brought in this world under these circumstances. All of this was given to me. So tell me why am I being talked about and being held responsible for something I had absolutely no control over? … Ignorance, point blank period! I loved my mother dearly, but we could not have been more different then night and day. One thing that I am a firm believer of is keeping marriage sacred. Now don't get me wrong, I'm not saying that I've never snuck around with somebody else's man or as everybody say today, been the side chick back in my younger days, because I would be lying... I'm not perfect... I'm only human just like everybody else. But what I can say is that I vowed to never do it again. Because when you think about it, what are you getting out of it? Whether he's a married man, or just somebody else's man? There's only two things you're promised to gain from it, and that's a bunch of unnecessary lies and a pair wet panties. I mean where can y'all go? What can y'all do? Because he's not about to jeopardize his relationship or his marriage by being seen in public with you. So that Olive Garden or seafood place that you love so much is out of the question, unless you're planning on going out to eat with one of your home girls. Oh yeah, and if you're ever in a jam... you may want to call someone besides him because you're on his time. So, if you have a flat tire on the interstate and you're depending on him, Sista girl you might as well consider yourself stuck like Chuck... depending on what time of the day it is. He's not about to get up from his dinner table with his family, out of his bed with his woman, or miss any of his children's games and practices for his side chick. Hunny Chile, don't you know that you can do so much better than that? I had to learn but I know I can! It's not even worth the headache nor the heartache. And besides, whenever I am blessed with a good man or a husband of my own, I don't want another woman fooling around with mine. I've learned that you will definitely reap what you sow.

But anyway, back to the subject at hand. Just because your mother had three kids by three different men or your father was an alcoholic, doesn't automatically means that one day, eventually, you're gonna be the same way. Girl, you can be whatever you wanna be if you apply yourself. We were all put here to serve a purpose. Don't ever let anyone discourage you or stand in the way of your destiny. Oh and trust me, they will try. People love saying, "she don't stand a chance", but that's so far from the truth. You do have a chance. You have just as good of a chance as anybody else. You have to push yourself, and really want it though. Whether you're studying to get your GED or studying to obtain your doctrine degree... GO GET IT! Absolutely NO EXCUSES! You can do it! And whenever you come across a stumbling block, get up, dust yourself off, and keep it moving girlfriend. You're not your mama, your grandmama, your sister, nor your aunt. You are your own woman! So girl you better own it! And don't ever let anybody tell you differently.

Attitude & Appearance

Attitude and Appearance both run together. If you think about it, most people base their first impression solely off of how you act and the way you look. Is it right? Ummm maybe not in some cases. They say never judge a books by its cover, but we do it anyway. Ladies and young ladies, I'm not trying to be mean in this chapter, but sometimes we do a little too much… I'm just saying! We see the video vixens on T.V., with the tight clothing, dancing around as if they got it going on. And they make it look so convincing and so easy with all the men and money but I'm here to tell you girlfriend that that ain't cute! It's demeaning, runchy, and unattractive. Parading around half naked in front complete strangers don't make you... sexy, appealing, or desirable. All it says is, 'look at me! Look at me! I'm easy and starving for any kind of attention that I can get. When in all honesty, it don't take all of that. If you want the world to treat you with respect, carry yourself respectfully. If you want to be recognized as a smart, intelligent woman, act like you got some sense. It's as simple as that! Always keep in mind that people will give you exactly what they get from you. And again, that has a lot to do with your attitude and your appearance.

When it comes to appearance, always dress in a way that not only compliments your body but most importantly is comfortable for YOU. When you leave the house comfortable in what you're wearing, you feel certain of yourself and that's a pretty great feeling. Now every woman has some place on her body that she's not to fond of. For me, it's my stomach area of course, after having three children. So, whenever I'm out doing a little shopping with my girlfriends, I buy blouses or shirts that doesn't cling to my midsection and something that's definitely long enough to cover it up! I wouldn't dare walk around a store showing the entire map of the United States spread across my belly in stretch marks. Ummm... can you say not funny at all! And definitely NOT CUTE! Well, I don't know, maybe it would be funny to all the innocent bystanders in the store who would be forced to witness it. I'm almost positive that they would rolling on the floor laughing at me. But I know better than to embarrass myself like that.

One day, last year, I went to pick my kids up from school early and when I got there, it was another parent there waiting to pick up her child. And y'all I am not trying to be funny and I swear I'm not making this up. It's 100% true! This woman had on a pair of black fished-net stocking, not leggings but stocking... there's a difference, with a pair of white panties underneath that were CLEARLY exposed, being that the black sleeveless shirt she was wearing stopped way above her waistline. On top of that, she had on house shoes! Nah girl, I hate to see a grown person out with their night clothes on or scarves on their heads. That's just the worst to me! UGH! But that's not even the worst part! To top it all off, she was every bit of 300 pounds... or more. And I could tell from her demeanor that she saw absolutely nothing wrong with what she had on. She thought it looked good. Smh... y'all if she wasn't embarrassed, I was definitely embarrassed for her because she looked absolutely ridiculous, bottom line.

Hunny Boo Boo, stop trying to keep up with everybody else. If you are a plus size woman STOP SHOPPING IN THE JUNIOR'S SECTION of the store because that's not your life. Go on over to your world and browse in the section that fits your figure. Don't get me wrong nah, I think ALL women are beautiful! I don't care what color, shape, form or size you are. We are just some beautiful creatures! But the number one way for a skinny sista to steal a big sista's shine is by that sista trying to wear her clothes. I mean, there is no other way to say it other than JUST DON'T DO IT!   Ok Ladies,

*** FASHION ALERT! FASHION ALERT! FASHION ALERT! *** FASHION ALERT! FASHION ALERT!***

1. If you have to tug or pull up your pants every time you stand up or change positions, then baby girl they're too small.

2. If when every time you bend over your breast are spilling out of your shirt and/or your bra, I'm sorry but that

needs to go. Again Sweetie, it's just too small and there is no way in the world that you can tell me it's comfortable.

3. Skinny sistas, just because you can put on just about anything and pull it off don't mean that you should. A lot of times less is more. You don't have to show off your belly every time you leave the house, even in single digit degree weather, or booty shorts when you have no booty at all LOLOLOL I'm just saying! But no, seriously y'all, it really don't take all that. If you're always dressing yourself in a way where your goodies are always being exposed, then that's all people are gonna see. So there is no need in getting mad and upset when you get that kind of attention, because that was your whole point in wearing it right? If your answer to that question is a "NO", then you wasn't comfortable dressing like that to begin with…. So yeah, with that being said, I guess that about sums up appearance huh!

Oh! Wait a minute, there's one more thing that I would like to point out. If you're somebody's mother dress yourself in a way where your children will be proud to say 'that's my momma.' Coming out of the house looking like you're headed to the club or looking like you just woke up and rolled out of bed… LITERALLY, is not only an embarrassment to yourself, but you're also embarrassing your child… Ok… carry on. *** SEE FASHION DO'S AND DON'TS ON PAGE 83 ***

ATTITUDE

All I have to say as far as attitude is to always try to be positive and be kind. A bad attitude will not get you anywhere. All it is, is a waste of energy that could be applied somewhere else. And it makes things a whole lot difficult for YOU. Not only does having a bad attitude almost always get YOU upset but it also play a big part in how the world perceives you. Nobody wants to be associated with, friends with or date a person who has a nasty attitude, and no one wants hire or give any opportunities to a person who always give the impression that they're nonchalant or angry for no reason at all. So, if you're gonna have a bad attitude, cause I know some people just can't help it, at least know when to turn it off! Again, it will not get you anywhere in life and it doesn't prove a thing other than the fact that you still have a lot of growing up to do. Grown women not only dress accordingly but they also act accordingly. Peace!

Find Your Own Groove
(Forget the Joneses)!!!

There's a lot of females out here who are more concerned about the next female instead of focusing on and trying to figure out what works for themselves. I know we've all heard the saying, "you don't have to do everything you see somebody else doing." And that's so very true. What's right for the next person may be all wrong for you hunny. Take for instance the natural look that's so popular today. Yes, it is a given that natural beauty is the most beautiful kind of beauty in the world but girl let's keep it real nah, it is not for everybody… I'm just saying. If you had hair that you could barely get a comb through when you were a child, what on earth makes you think you're gonna have any kinda "curl pattern" now??? I gotta know!!! So why do we do this? We do it to keep up with the joneses or maybe it's because we're not happy with ourselves and want to feel as though we belong. IDK! But those are the only two, most logical explanations I can come up with.

As I've stated a million times, I don't come from much and I never had a lot. So yeah, once upon a time I was that girl too. But hold up nah! Notice what I said! I said "girl." Ok… anyhoo…. I was that girl too. That girl who wanted to be "popular"… who wanted to belong. That girl who was so unsure of herself that she felt like she had to do what she saw everybody else doing to be accepted. That girl who believed that how a person looked or what a person was wearing made them somebody important… made them beautiful. I didn't feel like I looked good if my hair wasn't done and if I didn't dress a certain type of way I wasn't cute enough or old fashion. Bottom line, if I wasn't looking like what everybody else was looking like, I wasn't pretty and I didn't fit in. It was little things back then…. Now day's folks be trying to get implants and all that other nonsense to make themselves feel like they fit in with society. But that's a whole other book itself! Anyway, yep, I was her. Always second guessing myself. Second guessing was like second nature to me.

But one day, I think I was in about the sixth grade, one of my favorite teachers told me that I was beautiful. She said to me, "Brunwyn, but most importantly you're kind." She told me that having a kind soul is the most powerful beauty that one can have, and that that not only determines a person true beauty but also their importance to the people around them. And that's far more valuable then what someone is wearing or how a person looks. And then she asked me, "Have you ever looked in the mirror and stared into your own eyes?" Of course I hadn't. She said to me, "Just look at your eyes, they're beyond beautiful! They're gorgeous!" It wasn't until I was well on up in high school, but through my eyes I was able to find my own inner beauty, a beauty that once you truly find, nobody will ever be able to take it away from you.

Today, I look at my nine year old daughter and she's so much like me. A while back I even noticed that she'd started to second guessing herself a lot... just like I use to do LOL... what she wore, how she wore her hair. Y'all know kids these days start wayyyyy earlier than we did SMH! But anyway, so, I sat down with her and I told her to BE HERSELF… that it's ok to just be Rayla and that she should NEVER doubt who she is. Regardless to whatever happens in your life or what people say, it's important to NEVER forget who you are and where you come from. Because nine times out of ten those very people that you're trying to impression didn't come from no more then what you came from. So what makes them any better? I'll wait… my point exactly.

Now my daughter has a very vivid imagination just like her momma, so she usually never thinks within the box like the average person does. And once I gave her the "ok" to express herself, Baby, she did exactly that! Now she's always like Ma my friends are always fighting over who's gonna sit by me and who's gonna stand by me in line. She thinks she's "popular" LOL. But let me say this too, "popular" is a word that I absolutely hate! I explained to her, well to all my children, that being what your friends call "popular" is not what makes people like you. And how you dress or how you look doesn't make you a better person or a better friend, it's being yourself that does. Being yourself is what makes people appreciate you. However, she also knows that even still, being yourself is not a guarantee "friend catcher." There will still be people who will not like you, but that should never stop you from being who you are. So on the flip side, she also knows the importance of standing alone and that a leader doesn't have to keep up with everybody else, they march to the beat of their own drum. What I'm trying to say is love yourself. If there are some things that you don't like about yourself... change them or learn to love them. Find your own groove!

So listen up ladies, don't go out there trying to buy a bundle of Brazilian hair because your neighbor has some, when you know your child's birthday is right around the corner and right now you can only afford synthetic hair. Get your priorities in order Hunny Chile. Trying to keep up with the Joneses is only gonna break you. You'll never have a dime if you're spending trying to keep up with your home girl or trying to please society. Everybody's circumstances are different. Your home girl may have it like that. Either way, that doesn't mean that her beauty is out shinning yours. You're gonna always find somebody out there who you feel has more than what you got. But at the end of the day, NOBODY has it all, nobody's perfect… Actually, our imperfections are what makes us beautiful… they're what makes us who we are. So take what you got, and Sista WORK WITH IT! Now that some great advice for everybody huh… young and old?!? I'm soooo not the one who's interested in keeping up with the joneses. I honestly think it's kind of silly LOL. I'm perfectly ok with just being Brunwyn. I can't say this enough… confidence, confidence, confidence! Find your own groove girl!

Gotta Keep Those Priorities Straight

Keeping life in order can be a job itself. Now I've always been told that the woman has always been the backbone of every family… cooking, cleaning and nurturing… playing her role, the same role that most of us play every day. And trust me Hunny, I know it can be extremely overwhelming at times. That's why prioritizing is very important. Especially when you almost always have a zillion and one things going on at the same dang time. Now I know that we all have very different lives. The three duties that I have listed above are just the basics and far from what we do all day, every day. Some of you may include studying to that list. For others you may include working a 9 to 5.

For me, it's all of the above plus catering to four children and a dog. So you know there is never a dull moment in my day. And I mean that literally! I'm telling you, you may come to my house at any giving day of the week and be like, 'this woman is running a zoo.' Sometimes things can get beyond unorganized in my world. However, you better believe that no matter how unorganized things may be, my PRIORITIES are always going to be in line. Don't get me wrong now, we all get side tracked every once and a while, myself included. I mean it's bound to happen, again, we are not perfect creatures.

So with that being said, this chapter is strictly for the women and the young women who takes her pretty little time to bounce back. The ones who are almost away being thrown off of what she knows she needs to be doing for one reason or another. This is for the Sistas who puts their studies along with their grade point average on the back burner to party with the crowd every day of the week. Even though she's fully aware that completing college and obtaining her degree is her ticket to life she's always wanted. For that Sista who decided not to pursue college but instead she would go straight into the workforce, but has yet to find a decent job because for the life of her, she can't seem to get out of bed every day before 2:00 pm, and when she does she's too busy flooding everybody's Facebook and Instagram with her selfies.... Knowing good and darn well that she doesn't have anybody to support her but herself. Still she can't find the ambition to go out there and get that job, car and all the other essentials every independent woman needs. But she wants it. And last but definitely not least, this is especially for my Sistas who are mothers... single mothers out there who would rather chase in-behind one random Negro after the next instead of striving to provide a better life for her children. She can't ever find the time to make it to her son's parent teacher conference but will do whatever it takes to be able to stand in line to get that new IPhone or Jordans for the boo. Feeding her children Ramon Noodles and cereal but feeding her "man" chicken and steak... smh... kids bringing home "love packs" from school when she getting more than enough from the government to feed them. Not to mention they're wearing all the children in the neighborhood hand-me-downs. You know why? Because every penny she gets, she's spending it on one way or another to keep a man.

Ugghhh… just writing this is upsetting me, real talk. This kind of selfishness is just disgusting. Especially when you know that there is not a full time father figure in the home for the children. And I'm not going to say that not having a father present is ok but I know that it be like that sometime. However, when that's the case it just means that as a mother you have to stand stronger and work harder to ensure that you're providing a happy, healthy and stable environment for your children. I mean those are your responsibilities as a mother anyway. Your children and their stability should be your number one priority. And if your Bae don't understand that, then you don't need him anyway because he's just a child himself. Never neglect your kids for ANYONE, end of discussion. As mothers we should always live to provide a better life for our children than the life we had. They come first.

I'll be honest with you though. As far as everything else, like the slipping grades and the lack of ambition… between me and you, I've been there a time or two. My priorities weren't always straight. I went through that boy/man crazy faze like most young women do. So much so that my grades began to drop as well… they dropped so low that I decided to drop out of high school my senior year and get my GED. SMH… y'all have no idea how much that hurt my soul every time I think about it… "my GED." After all those years of going to school every day and getting good grades… at the very end I messed up and that cost me EVERYTHING I'd worked so hard for. I wouldn't be able to walk across that stage with my class. The class that I'd been with from the beginning… from kindergarten. I didn't understand how much that meant to me until after I realized that at that point, nothing I did or said could right that wrong. But again, I couldn't blame nobody but myself. I chose to sit my top priorities on the back burner and do what I wanted to do instead of doing what I knew I needed to be doing. And now I have to live with that for the rest of my life. For a long time I was too ashamed to even tell people that a GED was all I had. I was disappointed in myself. And that's because I knew that without a doubt I was more than capable of doing a whole lot better than what I did. But they say that there is a purpose to every failure. The fact that I did not get my actual diploma only made me go harder. I knew I had to do something. I had enough sense to know that a GED wasn't going to carry me and my baby very far. And like my good friend Antoneo "TK" King always told me, 'hunny when you know better, you do better!' Yessssssss! So that's exactly what I did! It took a little while but I searched my soul like a treasure chest until I finally found the ambition that I knew I'd had the entire time... I just didn't know what to do with it or how to use it. It took lots and lots of maturing and believing in myself. But look at me now! I mean, I hate to toot my own horn but BEEP BEEP baby hahahaaa! I've finished my second book and I'm currently writing my third! And who would've known that all it would take was a little prioritizing and believing in MYSELF.

As women we have to keep ourselves, our families and our lives in proper order by doing what we know is important, and doing it when it needs to be done. That alone will prevent a lot of unnecessary setbacks and careless mistakes. Sista girl, if you're in school keep those grades up... work hard, play harder! Ladies if you have children, take care of them for Christ sakes! You chose to have them, they didn't choose to be here. They come first.... before that man, before your hair, your nails... heck even before your own health! I know it gets hard and frustrating sometimes, especially when you're on your own, I swear I do! Having to get up with the birds every morning and drag four children out the house rain, sleet or snow to go to a job you absolutely hate just to make ends meet. Been there done that! Smh… Hunny, I get it if nobody else does. But it has to be done, and Sista you can do it by simply prioritizing and PRAYING! You shouldn't want your children, your neighbors, your friends… (Cause trust me your friends are talking about you too) society period, viewing you as anything less than a strong, beautiful, and independent woman with her priorities intact.

Know Your Worth

Who determines whether a woman is worthy or not? And no this is not a trick question….. Waiting…. The correct answer is SHE DOES. Ladies, if you don't know your worth how can expect anyone else to know it? Especially men! And I'm not saying ALL MEN… so let me clarify that, but most men can smell the fragrance of an insecure woman from a mile away. And they don't find it sexy or attractive, most will take advantage of it.

At 19 years old I fell "in love" for the first time. Now I know that most of my young Sista girls are probably wondering how I knew it was love… I didn't… and it wasn't. But being that I was still a baby and didn't know hardly anything about life I was made to believe that it was. And I swear y'all for a brief moment it actually felt like it really was love. After high school I moved to Chicago where I met him. The fact that we didn't know each other was a good thing and also a bad thing. The good part about it was the fact that we were both able to start from that moment... the moment that we met. Any and everything that happened before then was irrelevant because he didn't know me and I didn't know him. However, one thing that my momma always said was 'the same thing that will make you laugh will make you cry.' The bad part about it was that I was completely out of my element, and so far from my comfort zone with a complete stranger, trying to be grown.

Things were pretty good in the beginning. But isn't it always? I left my cousin's house, who l lived with in Chicago also, to go and live with him and his mama... SMH, to live with a man for the first time... at his mama's house... really SMH. Who does that??? But his mama loved me... or so I thought she did. Now looking back..., now that I'm older and is able to look at the whole situation from a grown woman's perspective, I'm not saying that she didn't like me but she definitely didn't love me. I honestly feel that she was more so of using me to keep her son out of trouble. I guess she figured that as long as she could keep me around he'd walk the straight and narrow, because gang banging and drug dealing is like second nature to young, black men in the windy city of Chicago. But boys will be boys and raising that man should've never been my responsibility… but hers. Besides, I was just a little country girl who had no clue as to who I was so what good was I to him. To be honest, at first I found it kind of fascinating… the fast money part anyway. He took care of me. Everything I needed he provided… food, money, and clothes, whatever. But Hunny, let me tell you… it wasn't worth it. Because anytime a guy, and again I'm saying most guys not all, is taking care of a female he also feels as if he is entitled to be in control of her and that relationship. And in my case it wasn't any different. He was taking care of me… my sole provider, so he expected me to do as he said… period.

I would stay in the house all day, keeping his mother company, while he ran the streets all day and hung out all night doing God knows what. But that wasn't even the worst part of it. I'd began to except the staying out part, I mean there wasn't nothing I could do about that anyway, but he started to take things further and starting getting completely out of control. He started talking to his mama any kind of way... I mean beyond disrespectful. That itself should have been a red flag for me to run like the wind because a man who will disrespect his mother don't have much respect for women anyway, but I was immature and just didn't know any better. So, I stayed there with him like his mama said I should do and he eventually became extremely aggressive towards me. His punching holes in the walls whenever he got angry, turned into him pushing me around. Didn't take me long to get sick and tired of that though and say screw it. However, the day I decided to leave and go back home to my momma and be the little girl that I had learned I was, he wouldn't let me go. He unpacked my things, looked me straight in the eye and told me that if I left he would kill his self. Now I had never heard anyone say anything like that and thought 'WOW'... would he really? Smh.... Again, his mother begged me to stay and I did. I stayed... mainly because I was afraid. Girl, I can't tell you how many times I laid in the bed with the cover over my head and silently cried myself to sleep. I still can't understand how a man can look into his woman's eyes and still raise his hand. I was miserable! So miserable that I had gotten to the point to where I just didn't care anymore. But in a weird sort of way I guess it made me a little bit braver. When he left, so did I. I could care less about what his mama or whoever else had something to say about it. Heck, she wasn't concerned about my well-being anyways. Because if she was she would've made me leave her house long before things had gotten that bad, instead of tricking me into staying every time. But like I said, her only concern was that he stayed out of trouble and out of jail. Guess she was just your typical mother trying to raise a man on her own with her own motives.

Every day, I would get up, get dress and hop on the bus and just ride. I never had any particular place to go, just needed to get away from them… needed a peace of mind. And every time I got on the bus all could I think about was my momma and how disappointed she would be in me if she knew how I allowed myself to be mistreated. Not to mention, the fact that I wasn't doing anything constructive. As a matter of fact, I was doing the exact opposite and there were so many opportunities up there! That made me sad, it made me feel worthless… HE made me feel worthless. And the fact that I felt so worthless made me disappointed in myself. I know to most of you this chapter of my book may seem pretty typical but I lived it and I take full responsibility for everything that I went through at this point in my life because I didn't have to live like this… I chose too… there's a difference. I knew my momma's door was always open for her children. As long as she had breath in her body we had a place to stay. But I was too young and too inexperienced to fully understand how messed up the entire situation really was. I figured it out real quick though… I bet you that!

Soon after, he got locked up and was held on drug charges. Hahaaaaa (not really funny though but I'm just being honest) and what you think I did? Uh yeah… I left!!! SEE YA!!! One thing these men need to understand is boo, if you wasn't good to me when you were free, what makes you think I'ma hold you down or be there for you while you're locked up? Boy BYE! Hunny, I didn't even tell his mama I was leaving. By the time they realized I was gone I was just touching down in Memphis TN. The whole ride home all kept hearing over and over in my head was what he had said to me a few nights before he was locked up. We were lying in bed and he rolled over and felt my pillow wet with my tear stains and said, 'love hurts... that's how you know it's really love.' NOT TRUE Sistas! The moment those words left his lips I knew that it was time for me to go. You see, I was always told that love didn't hurt and I don't think that my momma, someone who has loved me when nobody else did, would lie to me about something like that. I thank God that he had gotten locked up. I know that may sound harsh but that was my way out... the opportunity had presented itself and I took it. Had I not, I don't know what would've happened. But those are the chances we take when we try to grow up too fast.

Even though I never told my momma all that I had been through, I guess she could sense that something was wrong. Because after I got situated from the ride home, back to Oxford MS, she came in my room and sat next to on my bed, then she looked at me and said, " Flip, I know that you're not gonna tell me everything but a mother knows when her child is hurting." She told me that one day when I'm a mother I'll understand... she was right. Then she said, "I'm glad you came home and I want you to always remember that you are so much more than that."... Again, she was right. She then handed me this little pink mother-daughter book that I still have to this day and will one day give it to my daughter. It was open to a page that had the definition of self-worth printed on it, and it said, 'confidence in one's own worth or abilities; Self-respect.' I took the whole Chicago experience as a lesson learned and never looked back. Never once letting it break me or the knowingly fact that I am SO worthy.

Sistas, in every relationship you go into, let them know, let them sense how much confident you have in your own self-worth and they will always respect that in you. To all the mother's out there trying to raise your sons on you own, I take my hat off to you! I know it's hard but it can be done. Raise him to be a strong man who respects women, who loves and cherishes women and who's not just looking at them as an object or someone who's beneath him. He needs to know the importance of treating all women the same exact way he expects a man to treat you. And ladies, if you're in an abusive relationship, there are so many other options. So don't ever feel like you don't have anywhere to turn or that you have no choice but to lay down and take it. I'm talking physical and/or verbal abuse as well. Always know that you don't have to be anybody's punching bag or "self-esteem builder upper" (they wanna tear you down to feel better about themselves) because that's extremely unhealthy and a horrible way to live. So please, please, please consider removing yourself from that situation. I know it's easier said than done but you deserve and are so worthy of so much more.

For Me Or Nah

Life will place you in certain situations, good and bad to show you who's really FOR you. And you have to be very careful because some people will lurk around only to take from you. And when you don't have anything left to give, they're gone. One thing that I've learned is you can't make a person be FOR you. Either they are or they're not. So never waste your time stressing over it. If every person in the world that you come across was on your team, then hunny trust me you're not doing something right. So embrace you hater's compliments and keep right on winning!

Writing my first book, An Open Book of a Woman's Heart, was so not planned. It just kind of happened and is one of my greatest accomplishments. If nothing else, one day I will be able to tell my children and my grandchildren that I am an African American published author. However, you already know that where there's an up, there's a down. The sad part about writing my book was that it made me come to terms with the fact that a person I've loved for more than 12 years was not really FOR me. When I started writing my first book, I had no clue as to what to write about. Then I thought, LOVE. Everyone wants to be loved, right? So I started off with a short love story. After letting a few of my closest friends read it and convincing me how good it really was, I decided to writing a few more. And then I thought, 'hmmmmm… let me turn things up a notch or 10! What do people really like to read about? What sells? So I thought back to the books I'd recently read and was like…. Ummm SEX, INTIMACY, HEARTBREAK… Duh! I mean if you're gonna do something, why not do something that could potentially make you a couple of dollars? I don't know about y'all but I have four children so money definitely talks in my world! It made perfect sense to me.

Well this was a problem for many, the fact that I didn't let talking about sex intimate me. But what hurts the most is when the negativity is coming from a person you love. The 'why would you write that? What will your daughters think when they read it? Is this what you want people to remember by?' Geesh! Give me a break! My responses were, 'I'm going to continue to write about whatever I think will sell and will possibility provide a better life for me and my girls. I'm putting all intimation to the side. Secondly, my daughters are eight, nine, three and four. They have absolutely no business reading my book. Heck they don't even want to read the books that they have to read for school, let alone mine! Besides if ever they do read my book, they will be old enough to handle it, which will be a very, very long time from now. Lastly, all that I would hope people would remember me as would be a great writer. But I have no control of what people think. They will think what they want to think regardless so, I'm not going to lose any sleep over that part. All I can do is keep writing.

He didn't stop there though. Facebook became a huge problem. Even though he knew that it only pertained to advertising my book, he still had nothing but negative things to say. It doesn't take the smartest person in the world to know that communicating with your support group is essential when you're trying to get ahead. They are the one who are ultimately putting you out there. And I explained this to him. Bottom line, he just wasn't happy for me. Because if he was… if he was on my team, he would've said something like, 'even though I don't agree with the content of your book, because we're on the same team, I support you anyway.' I'm proud of you … something! But he didn't say that. Not even once. Instead, he flat out told me that he didn't support my book. And he frowned on everything in reference to my book, comments, pictures… everything. At first I stressed about it because this was something that I thought he'd be proud of, something we'd be able to enjoy together. After putting all that I had into producing my book, I thought he'd be the one who'd be my backbone. But it didn't happen like that. He changed up on me before I even realized it. So, I eventually washed my hands of the whole situation.

At this point in my life I'm cutting off the people who serves no purpose. I finally realized that he was just not FOR me, my accomplishments... Bosshia Rae period! No matter what I did or what I said throughout the entire 12 years, it just wasn't good enough for him. I was never right and he was never wrong. I heard from somewhere that any person who never sees the right in you will never see the wrong in themselves. And that's sooooo true. So in the end, I chose to keep writing for me and my girls and to stop fighting for someone who at the end of the day was just NOT FOR ME.

That Man, That Man Chile

I've been through some pretty interesting "relationships" with men as you can see from previous chapters. However it wasn't anything more than what I allowed. Most women want to be loved by somebody, anybody so bad that we force ourselves to be comfortable in "relationships" that we know are not healthy for us. We become more infatuated with not being alone verses whether or not this man really makes me happy. But why do we settle? Why do we take whatever a man dishes out? I'll tell you why, it because that's all we know how to do. We've never been taught how to be loved properly. And what a lot of parents don't realize is that the mentoring starts at home.

As young women and young girls the first thing we do is watch our mother and try to mimic everything that she does, how she walks, how she talks, how she laughs, and also how she cries. Then we watch our father to see how he treats our mother, do he make her laugh more than he makes her cry? And from that we start to get an understanding of what we are supposed to except as women and also how we're supposed to be loved and treated by a man. Whichever way, it will have an effect on the children of that household. If your daughter is not getting the proper attention, guidance and encouragement from dad or some type of a positive male figure, nine times out of ten she will go looking for it from whatever man she can get it from.

One thing that I've learned growing up and will pass on to my daughters, is that men will come a dime a dozen. A woman can get a man before she can come up with a dollar to buy a loaf of bread. And a dollar is not hard to scrap up… I'm just saying. So don't rush it and never settle simply because you're lonely, need sex, or because you just want to feel loved. So many of us women will accept any old kind of man and think we can change him. When in all actuality we should be changing our minds instead. We need to start refocusing our attention on bettering ourselves and our daughters. They're our future, the next generation and they need to know that opening their legs to every man who says I love you, WILL NOT keep him. However, keeping him chasing your assets will. **Assets**, meaning all the things you have to offer other than sex.

True, it's in our nature to love and desire men. And if you're anything like me, the blacker that man is the better Hunny hahahaha, but before you give him all that you have make sure he's the right man. What makes him the right man though? How would you know? In my 'Self-Worth' chapter I was just a baby but in this chapter Hunny I'm fully grown, so I'm going to tell you how you will know a good man, the right man. So ummm… little sistas you may wanna take notes boo.

First of all he needs to be a man who you are able to see potential in. If you don't see any potential in him then don't waste your time because he will only hold you back from reaching your highest potential. And don't ever let anybody stop you from shinning bright! A good man will be one who will be kind even when you're wrong. Not only will he see potential in your flaws, but your flaws will only make him love you more. A good man will never do or say anything to intentionally hurt you but instead he'll always be that someone there to heal you. He will support you and have your back through whatever. If you're in school he'll be that guy to stay up with you all weekend helping you crash for that exam first thing Monday morning, instead of keeping you up all night pacing because you haven't heard anything from him all weekend. For my sistas with children, he'll be some sort of father figure to them and wouldn't dare make any difference when it comes to his kids and yours. A good man will never allow his woman to ask another person for help, nor will he allow her to go without. He will always be right there to support her emotionally, physically and financially. And I'm gonna tell you a little secret, a real man will never hold a woman back for his own selfishness or games. If he's aware that he's unable to give her what she needs, he'll let her go.

Sistas, our man should be like our religion, the only thing that we believe in the name of love. If the connection is not that strong then reevaluate. Do whatever you have to do JUST DON'T SETTLE! Don't be out there wasting your time thinking he'll eventually get it together. And don't be out there competing with a million different women trying to prove a point. A man will only do what you allow him to do. But sistas it starts with us. Our daughters, nieces, sisters and our cousins are watching us even when we think they aren't.

So let's start setting a better example for them by getting our careers going, strengthen our religious beliefs instead of making it our New Year's resolution year after year. Let's start teaching them that being strong, being successful and respecting ourselves is what's really important. Men will come along in the process and you'll be surprised at how many you'll have to choose from after you're completely satisfied with self. Because then you'll have a lot more to offer other than your looks and your body (those things fade), but also an educated mind, your own money, a strong religious foundation and confidence! Now that's a tough woman to try to compete with and trust me, every man that crosses your path will also know that she's one he'll be a fool to let go of. So handle your business Sista girls! These men ain't going nowhere! They'll still be lurking when you're done!

Speak Up Girl

Grown women speak up. They say what they feel… period. If you like it, you like it. If you don't then that's cool too. However, a grown women don't speak ignorantly. And Girl, I know it can be challenging at times but trust me, it can be done without losing your voice. Sometimes we find ourselves in situations where your our patience is being tested. When in situations like these how do you handle it?

Let's say hypothetically you were in a situation where your boss just wouldn't cut you a break. Every step you make she's on your heels. Nothing you do or say is right and it's clear that when it comes to you she feels some kinda way. We've all been there but again I ask, how would you handle the situation? This chapter of my book was actually inspired by an incident that I currently witnessed at work.

Ok so… every morning I sat at my computer and watched my coworker walk in without a word and take her seat. Not a good morning, how you doing… nothing. It was clear to everyone who worked there that she and the supervisor wasn't too fond of each other… and that's ok! You don't have to sip tea with everybody you work with. But because my coworker didn't speak up, she was booted right out of the door. Now I'm going to tell you how she handled the situation girl, then I'm going to tell you how I would've handled it if I had to sashay in that sista's pumps Monday through Friday.

The first thing she did wrong everyday was come in and not speak. I get that you'd rather be quiet than be fake, but coming in and not saying at least 'hey', only proves that she does in fact have control over your day, your emotions, and your overall work performance. Sometimes you have to kill them with kindness. Don't ever let'em see you sweat! If it had of been me, I would've came in every morning and blessed her with my beautiful smile and last but not least, offered her the most polities good morning I had. Whether I was bothered by her or not she would've never known it. This is cold, cold world… you can't wear your heart on your sleeves or you'll never make it. Instead of asking the supervisor for help, she'd ask everybody but her… BIG MISTAKE! Hunny, there is work that comes with that title so whenever I needed help, I'd be calling the "Boss". That's what she's being paid to do, farther more, you don't intimidate me. Again, avoiding conversation with her only assures her that she has the upper hand of the whole situation. And that's something I definitely wouldn't give her the satisfaction of or anyone else for that matter. Umm yeah… professionally you may be the Head Boss in Charge but personally… nah. I'm sorry but there is nothing in this world another woman can do or say to upset me or intimidate me. I'm too grown for that. And if you don't understand where I'm coming from on that one, then you're not there yet.

I honestly think there was a power struggle between the two of them. Our "Boss" had just been recently promoted, but truthfully she was unqualified and was more enthused with the title. Walking around like everybody was supposed to bow down to her to keep their job. It's sad when people are given a little bit of authority and the abuse it because they aren't use to anything. She expected for everyone to tip toe around her without a word. But that's where I have to stop you right there. Regardless to who you may think you are, you're not gonna talk over me or talk to me any kind of way. Oh no, no, no! You don't have to like me but you will respect me. However, now that I'm grown I've come to realize that there is always a right way and there is a wrong way to go about handling every confrontation. So one particular day the supervisor called this young lady out on her job performance. Yep, in front of everybody instead of pulling her to the side or outside in the hall, which would've been the professional thing to do you'd think, and the girl retaliated…and it wasn't pretty. Keep in mind this young lady was young and nowhere close to being grown mentally. So I guess she handled the situation to the best of her ability. I can't repeat her words verbatim, all I do know is that she did let her know that if she'd been properly trained by her, then her work performance would've been better. And I agree. I could definitely understand her sticking up for herself. I would've done the same thing but I would've done it calmly and respectfully. Just keeping it real, that young lady was fired for speaking up for herself, and what else could you expect if someone puts you on blast in front everybody you work with. But she was told that it wasn't what she said, it was the way she said it... and I agree with that as well. However, in my opinion, I think that the real reason was the fact that Ms. "Bossy" had gotten a taste of her own medicine and was called out and she was embarrassed. LOL and everybody know you don't embarrass the BOSS!!! Girl, sometimes the best way to speak up for yourself is to not say anything at all. Now I know that may sound crazy but you don't have to waste your valuable time addressing or entertaining garbage. What this young lady didn't realize was that just like there were things expected from her as an employee, there were also things expected out her boss as well. And if she felt like she wasn't properly trained, then her boss wasn't doing her job and didn't meet expectations as a leader. Also, regardless to the fact that she was lead over our department, she has a boss as well. There is always a higher authority. She should've remained calm and cordial in front of us, her peers and continued to let Ms. Bossy thinks she was running something other than her shoes. Then walked right into HER (Ms. Bossy) boss's office with a pen and a legal pad... a couple witnesses too.

Hunny listen, people are gonna try you every day of your life... that's just what they do. But you just have to learn to pick and choose your battles. Most of the mess will not even be worth your time. However, whenever you find yourself in a place where you feel as if you're being singled out or disrespected, by all means SPEAK UP! Never allow anybody to walk all over you. Just do it respectably. A grown woman always shows the very best side of her, even at her worst.

That Girls A Boss

Ok ladies, sooooo in my last chapter I talked about trying to be the boss. But in this chapter we're going to talk about actually being the BOSS! Boss is a word that has been tossed a lot lately. Everywhere you go somebody wants to be a boss. But tell me this, what makes a woman a BOSS? Is it because her shoes are red bottoms or because she has men drooling at her feet every time she enters the room? NO! A boss is someone who takes care of business. She gets things done. She comes in all different shapes, colors, and sizes. But you will always be able to spot her out a crowd because everything about her will speak BOSS baby! With beauty she has brains. Yes she's very independent and she flaunts it! Anything less than that is what I like to call a BOSSETT… a boss in training! A boss don't need her Momma, Daddy, or baby daddy to support her because she got it like that! She always know how to act. She the best mommy to her children, a freak in the sheets with her man and one of the most intelligent , well educated, not to mention fabulous little chicks on the job. When she approaches you, she don't bite her tongue. She speaks up, never once allowing anybody to cause her step out of character or speak to loudly because she knows that it don't take all that to get her point across. And whomever she's talking to can tell from the look in her eyes that she absolutely does not have time for games. She means business. A boss keeps her chin up at all times. Even with the weight of the world on her shoulders you'll never know it. The pride in her step mixed with the smell of her perfume sends a vibe of no stress but complete control. Many may mistake her for being arrogant but she calls it confidence. Go on girl! Yep, she confident and proud of it thank you!

Anyway, so… now that we're all squared away on what a boss looks like. Let's play a game. Let's see if you ladies can distinguish whether or not that girl is a BOSS or a BOSSETT! Ok Girl, so…your home girl is driving a new 2014 Cadillac, but she's sleeping on your couch, her mama couch, her daddy couch… heck whoever's couch she can sleep on. Plus she's using her child support to pay the car note! …BOSS or BOSSETT? Ummm BOSSETT! Girl first of all, go get you own place. How are you gonna be driving a 2000 anything and you don't even have a stable place to lay your head at night. Sorry baby girl but you're not quite there yet. Moving along!

Ok, you see this college student one morning, who is also a single mom. You see her leaving her apartment headed to drop her kids off then to class in her dusty little red pinto. Later, you see her at your favorite restaurant waiting tables like she owns the place, I mean tips coming left and right. When she finally does clock out and make it home she has enough money in her apron to pay her bills for the month and enough money to get her and her babies back and forth from school and work for the rest of the week. BOSS or BOSSETT? Baby, that girl's a BOSS! She taking care of business! She could care less about keeping up with the latest. She has a plan and she's hungry to get there. She's making the best out of what she got because she know that bigger and better is soon to come. We see you girl! Keep doing your thing Boo!

Ok y'all, one more… the most typical one of all these days. This chick stay in the club but don't have a job. She has about three kids that may stay with here about three days out of the week, yet she walks around with her nose in the air like she's the finest thing in the world and everybody's hating on her, but will do anything to hustle up on a few dollars to pay her light bill before the 15th of the month. BOSS or BOSSETT? NEITHER! Girlfriend you're not even close. Here is what you need to do. I'ma need you to purchase one of my book, along with about ten other self-help books, go in your bedroom and close your door and don't come out until you have a new lease on life. Because nothing about you spell BOSS sweetie, I'm sorry to be the one to tell you. And I'm not trying to hurt nobody feelings… I'm just keeping it TRILL y'all. You either love me or you hate me, but hey at the end of the day it is what it is.

I stopped by the grocery store on my way home from work one day to pick up dinner for me and my kids, when I bumped into this sista. Well actually her three little girls and my four daughters were playing around in the restroom and that's how we started talking. When I say she was a boss up and down... I'm not lying. I give credit where credit is due. We looked to be around the same age. She may have been a year or so older. Anyway, our chatting about the girls turned into her telling me bits and pieces about her life. She was a single mother. She was telling me how she'd struggled most of her life, not to mention getting pregnant with her first daughter at a very early age. But even still, she always wanted to give her children a better childhood then she'd had. She told me that after struggling through college and all the long nights, she and her girls were finally in a good place. And y'all I didn't know the girl from Eve but her emotions were so real that I couldn't help but understand where she was coming from and to be happy for her. Hunny, her name tag read RN! And when we all left out the grocery store, Sista girl snapped all three of her girls in the back seat of her Benz and drove off!

A grown woman keeps the mindset of a BOSS. She's always proactive. She's a leader and has complete control over every aspect of her life. The phrase, 'by any means,' is just like gospel in her world, she lives by it. She know that she always has things to do and she don't trust anyone other than herself to get them done. There is no such thing as lounging. To all my Bossetts out there, keep moving forward, keep growing. Learn to lean and depend on yourself. I know it's always good to have a backbone but never make it your life line. Always stand strong and confident, doing what you have to do to make life comfortable for you and yours. Then girl, you too will one day be considered a boss lady. Who knows, maybe one day you'll even be a first lady! And to all my Boss Sistas out there, keep up the phenomenal work! You'll never go unnoticed! We see you girl!

Keep Squares Out Ya Circle

I've been told a time or two, that I'm just too nice. And that maybe true, but see the thing about me is I've always been the type of person who tries to give everybody a chance. Most times I try to give even the people who hurt me the benefit of a doubt at least once, when in all honesty I probably should've dismissed them right from the start. Because if a person burn you one time… they'll burn you again. Regardless, there comes a time where you have to face reality. Especially when it comes to the word "friend." I had to learn the hard way that not everyone who claims to be your friend, and I use that word loosely, is actually your friend. Sometimes your sister has to be your best friend.

Every person that you allow in your circle has some kind of intentions. You have to be the one to determine whether or not those intentions are good or bad, real or fake. Girl, this is something that I struggled with for a long time. Until I learned that not every person who you come across or cross paths with is meant to stay in your life. That goes for male and female. And I'm going to tell you this, if at any point you ever have to question a person's intentions, or their loyalty, hunny that is not your friend. Real, genuine friends are hard to come by, so if you're ever blessed with any, cherish them.

There was this girl, that I was never really close to, but she seemed like a nice enough person, so I tried to develop a friendship with her, which even shocked me, because everyone who knows me, knows that I don't do new friends. Anyway, I went above and beyond for this girl. I can't even count the number of times, that I sat listening to her men problems, and whatever else she had going on. But eventually, I started to notice that whenever I had something on my mind, she was one of those people who was never available. It was always either, girl let me call you back, or she would find some kind of way to turn the conversation so that we would end up talking about her issues. So of course that left me questioning her intentions. The more and more I listened to this chick, the more I knew for sure that this was a one sided friendship, and she was not my friend. Like my Aunt Renee always say, with her crazy self, 'just because I'm a friend to you, don't mean you're a friend to me.' So I distanced myself from her. Didn't work though, because she just started showing up at my house unannounced whenever I didn't answer my phone. Crazy right? Lol. But I fixed her. Every time she would call, I wouldn't answer, then I would close and lock my front door. Girl bye! Ain't nobody got time for that! But this is why I say I'm too nice. Even though I knew she was a snake in the grass and would forever remain categorized as an associate in my book, an extra in my play, or whatever you want to call it, I still tried to be nice when she desperately needed a job. So I helped her out and got her a job where I worked at the time. I figured, she'd never done anything to hurt me, and we don't necessarily have to be friends to work together. So I'm like what the heck, she needed it, and I would want someone to do the same thing for me if I was in her situation, and I went against my better judgment, only for her to come on the job, and start up a ton of drama and mess. Always, and I do mean always go with your first mind. If you feel so strongly about something, then girlfriend you should probably go with your first thought. Don't second guess it. She didn't have a car and just as I suspected, on Sunday she showed up at my door as if we were BFFs. Girl, my momma didn't raise no fool! What she needed was a ride back and forth to work… Duh! Now listen, most of the time I am quiet and to myself, however, if I feel you're being fake I will definitely let you know. And I made no exceptions for her. I went ahead and gave her a ride but I told her that I don't have time to play pretend. And that I didn't consider us friends and that that was OK. She didn't have to come to my house like we were. I explained to her that I helped her get the job but it was her responsibility to keep it and that I have four children of my own that has to be somewhere every morning, so I couldn't be dropping off hers. Now all of a sudden, "Brunwyn I always consider you as a friend. Sorry if I haven't made you feel that way and a blah, blah, blah and a yeah, yeah, yeah." And there I went, second guessing myself yet again… SMH. Thinking maybe she's right, I do work a lot and hardly made myself available for anyone. So I thought... yeah, maybe it was partly my fault.

But Anyhoo, to make a long story short I ended up letting her car pool back and forth with me for about two weeks. And in those two weeks not only did she not put a penny of gas in my tank but she also stirred up a whole bunch of mess on the job. Yep, every conversation that we'd had in the car to and from work, she went right back and repeated everything I SAID about this and that but forgetting to tell anything she'd said and how she'd initiated 99.9% of every conversation. I'm this kind of person, if a conversation is started and I overhear it... I might put my two cents in it and keep it moving. But I am NEVER the one to just sit up and talk about other people. I'm sorry but I just don't care that much. I got way too much going on in my life then to be worrying about somebody who ain't paying my bills. I mean, I just can't. I'll leave that to the people who don't have anything to do all day long. And just being honest, every conversation we had consisted of her asking me about this person or that one. I'd been on that job for two years, so I knew the ropes of survival. And I would tell her exactly what the supervisor told me... keep to yourself and do your job, stay away from this person, that person you could learn a lot from, things like that. Thinking she'd be smart enough to use it to her advantage, so she'd be able to upgrade from a temp to permanent. MY MISTAKE! And let me say this also, her going back being MESSY and running her mouth didn't make me a bit of difference. I stand behind everything I say PERIOD. And it will not change whether you like it or not. All of this was my fault though y'all. I take full responsibility and don't blame nobody but myself because I knew better! It wasn't just a coincidence that she just so happen to be with messy people every time I saw her, she was just as messy as they were… she just did a better job at hiding it. I've started to notice that I am like my momma in so many ways, yet so different. But like she always use to say, "I have ZERO TOLERANCE for drama." So at the end of the day, she was dismissed AND she got fired on top of that. BYE BYE GIRL! Simple as that.

Now on another note, too, I've been in a situation sooooo similar to this but it wasn't as easy to let go of. There can be people in your life, that you've known and loved forever, but if they are not meant to remain in your life, then that's just what it is. This girl and I went wayyyy back. We have slept in the same bed together, sang together, even cried together. She had always been like a sister to me. I honestly cannot tell you what went wrong, we just stopped talking. But whatever the reason is, I'm not questioning it. I feel like if you really consider a person to be a friend, then that's the way it will always remain. Friends talk about their problems, no matter what it is, especially when it puts their friendship/relationship in jeopardy. If somebody is feeling some type of way, they come to the other person, like grown women do, and hash it out among themselves. They don't send silly little text messages, and go on Facebook expressing their feelings to the world. They go to that friend with respect, and hear each other out, then make their decision on which way to go with that friendship based on their private conversation. All that other mess is just what I said... MESS and CHILDISHNESS, and Bosshia Rae ain't got time for that! If you don't even have the decency or guts to come to me like a grown woman, then hunny this "friendship" is so not worth my time nor my energy. As I stated earlier I have way too much other stuff going on, to be pacifying another "grown woman"

LOL. And even though I hated it, I dismissed her.... PERIOD. She needed to find herself anyway. I think that was the real issue. And to be honest, I haven't missed a beat! And the fact that I knew that I hadn't done anything to her, other than be a friend, made it a whole lot easier to let go.

Life goes on with or without. And people like that, only make you appreciate the real friends that you do have. The ones that not only talk…but listens, the ones that come over to house and eat up all your food then take a nap on your couch, the ones that borrows your things and keep them, the ones who's there when you're happy and cry with you when you're hurting, the ones that will be there regardless. No friendship is perfect. But the people in your life who realizes that and still stick around, are what you call true friends, your LOYALS. And in my case, ladies you know who you are! So choose your friends wisely, and always surround yourself with positive, like-minded individual. Oh yeah, and keep those squares out yah circle!

Picking Up The Pieces

Picking up the pieces is my most personal chapter of this book. This chapter is very near and dear to me. Like I've said so many times before, I didn't come from much. The most valuable thing I've ever had in my life was my momma. She taught me everything I know. My sense of humor, my wisdom, and my independence… all comes from her, Arness Faye Ivy. I know she may not have meant a lot to most of you who are reading this book, if you knew her, but she meant the world to me. She was all I had… and when she passed away I became numb to a lot of things. A lot of things that use to matter to me became irrelevant. And there is no one or nothing in this world that could hurt me as much her death hurt me, no matter what they do or say... nothing. Have you ever heard that saying about being so down that you have no other choice but to come up? Well, I've been there, done that and wore the t-shirt.

However, at this point in my life I didn't think that I would ever get back up. Every time I tried, I got knocked right back down. All I could do was cry. But guess what, I overcame it all. It took me some time but with prayer and help from my sisters and my aunt I was able to stand. And right now, today, at this point in my life, I'm stronger than I've ever been. I have strength that I never even dreamed I had. And nothing or nobody can break me.

I'll never forget that day... my momma called me, she had just gotten off work, and she said to me, "Flip, I fixed the kids a burger and some fries, and I'm sending my last $15.00 to you so you can order Smoochie's (my niece) birth certificate." That was the very last time I heard my mother's voice. If only I'd known that that would be the last time, I would've picked her up from work that day like I always did instead of sending someone else to go get her... regardless to how tired I was. I would've said my goodbyes instead of mumbling, "Ok Ma, alright Ma," but I didn't know. About an hour after I talked to her, my cousin called me and told me she'd stop breathing. That one phone call changed my whole, entire life. I hopped up out of my bed. I had my five year old daughter at the time, Rayla with me. I had my five month old daughter Raegan on my hips, and I was almost five months pregnant with my baby, Jeryah. I got there as fast as I could… but unfortunately, she was pretty much gone. Her neighbor was there preforming CPR, but I knew that there was no hope when my face touched hers. That was the saddest, most devastating thing I've ever had to go through. To sit there and watch the only consistency in your life take their last breath is beyond heart breaking.

So many thing raced through my head after we buried my momma. Mainly thing like coping and surviving. Trying to pick up the pieces and cope with everyday life without her was extremely hard and stressful because I still needed her. And now I had three daughters because I had to take my nieces in and become her legal guardian, she had to have some where to go. And my momma always told me that if something ever happened to her to take my niece and let her continue to grow up with Rayla… so that's what I did, plus I had a baby on the way. So yeah, surviving, trying to budget our monthly expenses seemed impossible. And just when I thought thing couldn't get any worse, about a month after my mama passed I lost my job. It was in August 2011, I woke up one night, soaking wet, thinking Lord did my water break? So I hurried up and stumbled on in the bathroom to check myself, but to my surprise it was worst, it was blood EVERYWHERE! My doctor diagnosed me with placenta previa. Placenta previa is a condition caused by a low lying placenta. It happens when your placenta is laying so low in your uterus that it covers your cervix and it causes a whole lot of bleeding. I was placed on strict bed rest for the remaining four and a half months of my pregnancy, so I was forced to resign. I honestly didn't think I was gonna make it. Not only did I have to resign from my job, but I also had to split my kids up. They couldn't stay with me because I couldn't take care of them. I couldn't get out of bed to feed them or get them ready for school every morning. I couldn't even lift my baby, Raegan. It was strictly bathroom, couch or bed for me. I was so down and so depressed. I just wanted it to be all over, until that one day when I started bleeding uncontrollably and had to have an emergency C-section two and a half months early... then I wished I hadn't said that. My baby weighed only three pounds and was so premature that the hospital here in Oxford couldn't do anything for her. I was so exhausted and tired from all the blood lost and transfusions that I vaguely remember them rushing her out the door. All I remember the pediatrician saying was that he didn't give up on her, but due her not breathing the first 16 minutes of her life, it was unclear as to how much, if any, brain damage was done... and only time would tell. My baby was in the hospital in Tupelo for little over a month. But she beat all odds.

It was definitely a struggle for me at this point in my life. Everybody near and dear to me was out of my reach. And when I say I was broke, I was broke. I can't even began to tell you how my baby's father and I made it back and forth to Tupelo every day to visit Jeryah Arness, but we did. We rolled up a lot of change LOL SMH... but we made there and back every day that she was there without asking anybody for anything.

So anyway, things started to eventually get better. All of my kids were back at home and even though I didn't have a job… we were surviving and coping the best that we could. Then out of nowhere came this excruciating headache that lasted for a week before I finally decided to go see a doctor. And they told me had an arachnoid cyst on my brain… SMH. I just felt like I couldn't catch a break. It was one thing after another. I'm thinking, why is all of this happening to me and why NOW? I have four little girls that need me… they don't have anybody else and I can't win for losing. I didn't have my momma to run to. I didn't know what to do. And baby, when I tell you I cried and cried and I cried… Until one day my aunt called me, Lord rest her soul, and she told me that I had to get myself together. She told me that all of this was just a test. She said that my momma always told her that out of all her children I was the strongest and that the Lord wouldn't put no more on me than I could bear. And I'ma tell you something, I stumbled and I cried so many nights but I knew I had to make it. I didn't have a choice. I had to make it for my daughters.

Eventually I got to the point to where I could stand without wobbling. All the pain and disappointment I used as stepping stones and I never looked back. I have the most awesome job in the world now, PLUS I'm a published author! My kids are happy and have everything they need. And that's enough for me because I've never been high maintenance anyway. In my 32 years I've learned that life is just a test. And the ones who are able to embrace their struggles and pick up the pieces… are considered the strong ones…the ones who survive. And guess what Sista, I'm still surviving and so can you. And if I can help you in ANYWAY along the way, then that's what I'ma do!

I'm Just Saying Sista Girl II

I've been through some pretty tough times in the last few years. Yep, I must say that I have. But somehow in the mist of it all… I made it. I'm so far from where I was, yet still so far from where I wanna be. I hope that every sista who reads this book can get at least something from it. It is aimed to educate my younger Sista Girls and to also uplift, encourage, and empower my Sistas of all ages. I have four daughter, so I'm all FOR woman and us making it! And I just want you all to know that you can do it girl, while looking absolutely fabulous in the process! Love you Sistas!

Bosshia

Fashion Dos and Don'ts

*** If it too tight take it off!

*** If it's falling off of you take it off!

*** If you are a plus size woman DO NOT shop in the juniors section and vice versa!

*** A lot of times less is more (this applies to makeup and accessories)!

*** Just because you got it doesn't mean you have to always flaunt it!

*** Wear things that will insinuate your body type!

*** And MOST importantly, you should feel comfortable and confident in whatever you're wearing!

A Gift From Bosshia (Just Write)

Like most Sistas, I keep up with the most important events, goals and emotions in my life through journaling. Not only is it a stress reliever for me, but it's also one of the best ways to keep track of my personal growth, which is so important because you always wanna strive to be better. You can't see how far you've progressed if you don't remember where you've been. So, I've provided you with your very own starter journal that you may use to express yourself! Use it openly nah! Because every woman has a story to tell… So go on girl, JUST WRITE.

BE BLESSED!!!

Just Write

Just Write

Just Write

Just Write

Just Write

Just Write

Just Write

Just Write

Just Write

Just Write

Just Write

Just Write

Just Write

Just Write

Just Write

Just Write

Just Write

Just Write

Just Write

Just Write

Just Write

Just Write

Just Write

Just Write

Just Write

Just Write

Just Write

Just Write

Just Write

Just Write

Just Write

Just Write

Just Write

Just Write

Just Write

Just Write

Just Write

Just Write

Just Write

Just Write

Just Write

Just Write

Just Write

Just Write

Just Write

Just Write

Just Write

Just Write

Just Write

Just Write

Just Write

Just Write

Just Write

Just Write

Just Write

Just Write

Just Write

Just Write

Just Write

Just Write

About the Author

Bosshia Rae is the author of the steamy, romance book of short stories, *"An Open Book of a Woman's Heart."* She currently resides in Oxford Mississippi with her four daughters, where she's working on her new upcoming book of short stories and say's her urge to write comes from her desire to read.

Where to find me

Add me on Facebook @ Facebook/Bosshia Rae

Also LIKE Bosshia's Book Club on Facebook

Follow me on InstaGram @ Bosshia Rae

Checkout my website where you can also purchase books by Bosshia Rae @ www.booksbybosshiarae.com

www.ingramcontent.com/pod-product-compliance
Lightning Source LLC
Chambersburg PA
CBHW061656040426
42446CB00010B/1770